FRONT-END
LOADERS

by Aubrey Z

Cody Koala

An Imprint of Pop!
popbooksonline.com

abdobooks.com
Published by Pop!, a division of ABDO, PO Box 398166, Minneapolis, Minnesota 55439. Copyright © 2020 by POP, LLC. International copyrights reserved in all countries. No part of this book may be reproduced in any form without written permission from the publisher. Pop!™ is a trademark and logo of POP, LLC.

Printed in the United States of America, North Mankato, Minnesota

052019
092019

THIS BOOK CONTAINS
RECYCLED MATERIALS

Cover Photo: Tech. Sgt. Erik Gudmundson/PJF Military Collection/Alamy
Interior Photos: Tech. Sgt. Erik Gudmundson/PJF Military Collection/Alamy, 1; iStockphoto, 5, 7 (top), 7 (bottom left), 7 (bottom right), 8, 11, 14, 16, 17, 19 (top), 19 (bottom left), 19 (bottom right), 20; Shutterstock Images, 13

Editor: Meg Gaertner
Series Designer: Sophie Geister-Jones

Library of Congress Control Number: 2018964598
Publisher's Cataloging-in-Publication Data

Names: Zalewski, Aubrey, author.
Title: Front-end loaders / by Aubrey Zalewski.
Description: Minneapolis, Minnesota : Pop!, 2020 | Series: Construction vehicles | Includes online resources and index.
Identifiers: ISBN 9781532163340 (lib. bdg.) | ISBN 9781644940075 (pbk.) | ISBN 9781532164781 (ebook)
Subjects: LCSH: Loaders (Machines)--Juvenile literature. | Excavation--Juvenile literature. | Construction equipment--Juvenile literature. | Construction industry--Equipment and supplies--Juvenile literature.
Classification: DDC 621.8--dc23

Hello! My name is

Cody Koala

Pop open this book and you'll find QR codes like this one, loaded with information, so you can learn even more!

Scan this code* and others like it while you read, or visit the website below to make this book pop.

popbooksonline.com/front-end-loaders

*Scanning QR codes requires a web-enabled smart device with a QR code reader app and a camera.

Table of Contents

The Front-End Loader Can Help!

Workers need to clear a pile of dirt. A front-end loader scoops up the dirt. It pours the dirt into a dump truck. The dump truck carries the dirt away.

Watch a video here!

Chapter 2

A Front-End Loader's Job

Front-end loaders clear areas. They lift and carry **loads**. These loads include rocks, dirt, and snow.

Front-end loaders are also called front loaders, wheel loaders, or loaders.

Learn more here!

Front-end loaders can also dig. But they can't dig very deep. People use front-end loaders in farming, construction, and **mining**.

Chapter 3

Parts of a Loader

A front-end loader has several parts. The driver sits in the **cab**. The driver can control the loader's movement. Most loaders move on wheels.

Complete an activity here!

The **bucket** carries the **load**. Different buckets help with different jobs. Some buckets move sand. Others move trash.

bucket

bucket lever

cab

lift arms

wheels

The **lift arms** extend from the cab. They lift and lower the bucket. A **bucket lever** moves the bucket forward and backward.

First, the bucket lever tips the bucket backward. The bucket scoops up a load.

Then the lever tips
the bucket forward. The
bucket pours out the load.

Chapter 4

Types of Loaders

Front-end loaders can be big or small. Big loaders are used for **mining**. Small loaders are used for yard work.

Learn more here!

A **backhoe** loader has a
shovel on the back. It can dig
deep holes.

People can turn their tractors into front-end loaders. They can attach **lift arms** and **buckets** to the tractors.

The Rook is a loader that helps police officers fight crime. It can break down doors and move cars.

Making Connections

Text-to-Self

Have you ever seen a front-end loader? What job was it doing?

Text-to-Text

Have you read about other construction vehicles? What are the different jobs that they can do?

Text-to-World

Front-end loaders come in different sizes. Why do you think that might be helpful?

Glossary

backhoe – a machine that digs by pulling a bucket backward through the ground.

bucket – the part of a loader that carries things.

bucket lever – the part of a loader that connects the lift arms and the bucket.

cab – the part of a vehicle where the driver sits.

lift arm – one of two long bars that move a loader's bucket up and down.

load – the object that is being carried.

mining – the process of digging rocks or minerals from the ground.

Index

Online Resources

popbooksonline.com

Thanks for reading this Cody Koala book!

Scan this code* and others like it in this book, or visit the website below to make this book pop!

popbooksonline.com/front-end-loaders

*Scanning QR codes requires a web-enabled smart device with a QR code reader app and a camera.